Spotter's Guide to
THE
SEASHORE

Su Swallow

Illustrated by John Barber

with additional illustrations by Joyce Bee,
Trevor Boyer and Christine Howes

Special Consultants: Christopher Humphries,
Ian Tittley,   Shirley Stone, Paul Cornelius, Kathie Way,
Ailsa Clark, Ray Ingle, David George,
Alwyne Wheeler, and Martin Sheldrick of the British
Museum (Natural History), London; and
Peter Holden, National Organizer of the Young
Ornithologists' Club.

Contents

Designed by
Sally Burrough and
Valerie Sargent

Edited by
Sue Tarsky and Jessica Datta

First published in 1978 by
Usborne Publishing Limited,
20 Garrick Street, London WC2

Text and Artwork © 1978 by
Usborne Publishing Limited

Printed in Great Britain

The name Usborne and the device   are
Trade Marks of Usborne Publishi n   Ltd

How to Use this Book

This book is an identification guide to the wide range of animals and plants that you can find on the seashore. Take it with you when you go out spotting. The species (or kinds) of animals and plants in the book are divided into the groups they belong to, and you will find sections in the book on seaweeds, birds and fishes, as well as sections on more unusual animals like sea slugs and sponges.

The description next to each illustration tells you points to look for and will help you to identify the species. Some species have no common English name. In these cases, the names are in Latin.

Next to each description is a small blank circle. Each time you spot a species, make a tick in the correct circle. The scorecard at the end of the book gives you a score for the species spotted. A common species scores 5 points and a very rare one is worth 25. You can add up your score after a day out spotting.

Page	Species	Score	Date May 2	Date June 1	Date
7	Yellow Horned Poppy	15	15	15	
7	Sea Kale	25	25		

Scorecard

Areas Covered by this Book

You can use this book as a guide to the seashore life of all the yellow areas shown on the map. Some of the species in the book are very rare in Britain, or are not present at all. These species are common in other European countries, so you can try to spot them if you go abroad.

Where to Look

There are four main kinds of beach: rocky, sandy, muddy and shingle. The kind of seashore life you spot will vary from one to another, although some species live on all kinds of beach. The descriptions tell you on which kind of shore each species lives.

Many of the species live on the shore or in shallow water. Others, like the jellyfishes, live in the sea, but can be spotted washed up on the beach. A few, such as the dolphins, swim close enough to be spotted from the shore. Look on cliffs for birds and plants, and in rock pools for sea anemones and fishes. You can also find seashore life, particularly birds and plants, on saltmarshes and estuaries.

Rocky Shores

Rocky shores are ideal habitats for many seashore plants and animals. Shells hide in crevices, seaweeds cling to the rock surface, fishes and crabs hunt for food in the pools. Look for flowers along cliff tops.

Tides

The tides are caused by the positions of the moon and sun in relation to the earth. The sea comes up and goes down the beach twice every day, so there are two high tides and two low tides. About every two weeks, it comes up higher and goes down lower than usual. These tides are called **spring tides** (nothing to do with the season). Small tides, called **neap tides,** occur in the weeks between the spring tides. Between neap and spring tides, the tides steadily increase and decrease. (The Mediterranean Sea only ever has a very small tide.)

Before you go out, find out from the local paper when the tides are.

Zones

The area between the low water lines of spring and neap tides is called the **lower shore,** and the area between the high water lines of spring and neap tides is called the **upper shore.** The main part of the beach, between these two shores, is called the **middle shore.** If you know when the spring tides are, you can explore the lower shore. The descriptions in this book refer to these three areas, so you will find it useful to know them when you go out spotting.

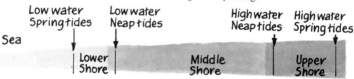

Sea
Low water Spring tides | Low water Neap tides | High water Neap tides | High water Spring tides

Lower Shore | Middle Shore | Upper Shore

Sandy and Muddy Shores

Sandy and muddy shores are good places to look for wading birds and gulls that come to feed on the molluscs and worms that live buried under the surface. Fishes often swim in the shallow water. Many plants grow on sand dunes high up on the shore.

Shingle Shores

Little can grow on a shingle beach, because the pebbles are always being moved by the sea and do not hold water when the tide is out. Look for seaweeds and empty shells washed ashore. You may find barnacles and mussels attached to breakwaters.

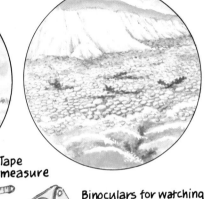

What to Take

If you study sea-shore life, you will need to take equipment with you. The most important thing is a notebook and pencils to record the species you find. Always make a note of the date and the place where you found the specimen. You can put your book in a plastic bag to keep it from getting wet. These pictures show some other things you will find useful.

When you've finished looking at an animal, put it back where you found it. If you move rocks or stones to look under them, put them carefully back in position. Handle all animals with care.

Tape measure

Binoculars for watching birds, seals and porpoises

Magnifying glass for looking at small animals and flowers

Shrimping net for exploring rock pools

Clear plastic box for looking in rock pools

Bucket for specimens

Sieve for finding animals buried in sand

Plastic bags for shells, pebbles and seaweed

Measuring Plants and Animals

The descriptions of the plants and animals in the book tell you their sizes. They are not drawn to scale. This page shows how they are measured and will help you when you're identifying something. Some species, such as fishes, are difficult to identify because their colours can vary. Measuring species with a tape measure will help you to identify them, but remember that young ones will be smaller than the average fully-grown ones.

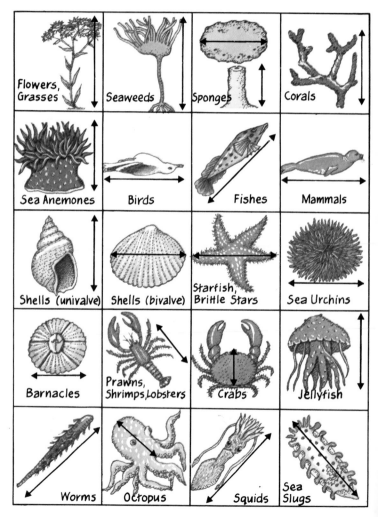

Flowers, Grasses

Seaweeds

Sponges

Corals

Sea Anemones

Birds

Fishes

Mammals

Shells (univalve)

Shells (bivalve)

Starfish, Brittle Stars

Sea Urchins

Barnacles

Prawns, Shrimps, Lobsters

Crabs

Jellyfish

Worms

Octopus

Squids

Sea Slugs

Flowers & Grasses

Look for flowers on shingle and sandy beaches, cliffs, dunes and saltmarshes.

Pod

Yellow Horned Poppy ▶

Called Horned because of the long green pods, which appear in summer. Flowers June-Sept. Shingle beaches. Up to 1 m tall. ◯

Leaf

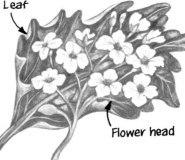

Flower head

◀ Sea Kale

Grows in clumps on shingle. Broad, fleshy leaves have crinkly edges. Flowers June-August. Up to 1 m tall. ◯

Golden Samphire ▶

Stout plant with shiny, fleshy leaves. Often grows in large clumps on saltmarshes, shingle and cliffs. Flowers in autumn. 60 cm tall. ◯

◀ Sea Sandwort

Also called Sea Purslane. Common creeping plant on loose sand and shingle. Helps to stop sand drifting. Flowers May-August. 30 cm tall. ◯

To identify the flowers you find by the sea, notice the shape of the plant and its leaves, and the kind of place where it grows.

◀ Sea Holly

Prickly plant with clusters of tiny flowers, which attract butterflies. Its thick leaves turn white in winter. Sand and shingle. Up to 50 cm tall.

Flower spike

Sea Wormwood (left) ▶

Strong-smelling plant. Leaves are downy and greyish. Grows above high tide level in estuaries. Up to 50 cm tall.

Sea Centaury (middle) ▶

Grows on dunes and sandy places near sea, but not widespread. Clusters of flowers in July and August. Up to 25 cm tall.

Marram Grass (right) ▶

Common on sand dunes. Its long roots and leaves trap sand and stop it blowing away. Flowers July and August. Up to 1.2 m tall.

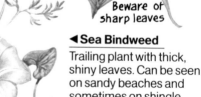

Beware of sharp leaves

◀ Sea Bindweed

Trailing plant with thick, shiny leaves. Can be seen on sandy beaches and sometimes on shingle. Look for the flowers from June-Sept.

Flowers & Grasses

Tiny flowers

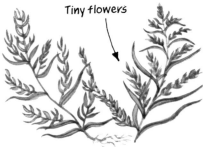

Annual Seablite ▶

Grows along the ground or upright. Clusters of tiny green flowers appear at base of upper leaves July-October. Saltmarshes. 20 cm tall.

Downy leaves

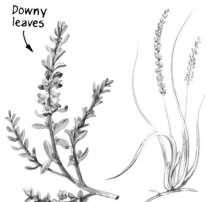

◀ Sea Milkwort (left)

Creeping plant that spreads over grassy saltmarshes. Flowers June-August.

◀ Sea Arrow-Grass (right)

Tough plant with flat sharp leaves. Flowers May-Sept. Grassy saltmarshes. 15-50 cm tall.

Sea Lavender (left) ▶

Tough, woody plant with leaves in a clump near the ground. On muddy saltmarshes. Flowers July-Sept. Up to 40 cm tall.

Sea Aster (right) ▶

Flowers in late summer, with mauve or white petals. Saltmarshes. Up to 1 m tall.

Flowers & Grasses

Thrift or Sea Pink (left) ▶

Grows in thick cushiony tufts on rocky cliffs. Look for the flowers March-Sept. 15 cm tall. ◯

Sea Mayweed (right) ▶

May be creeping or upright. Feathery leaves are fleshy. Daisy-like flowers. Grows on cliffs. Up to 60 cm tall. ◯

◀ Bird's Foot Trefoil

Bright yellow flowers streaked with red. Seed pods split and curl when ripe to release seeds. Grassy banks and cliffs. 10 cm tall. ◯

Pods

Buckshorn Plantain (right) ▶

Hairy leaves grow from a point close to the ground. Look on gravel near the sea. Spikes of flowers May-October. 10 cm tall. ◯

Sea Campion (left) ▶

Common on cliffs and shingle beaches. Spreads to form cushions. Flowers June-August. 20 cm tall. ◯

Seaweeds

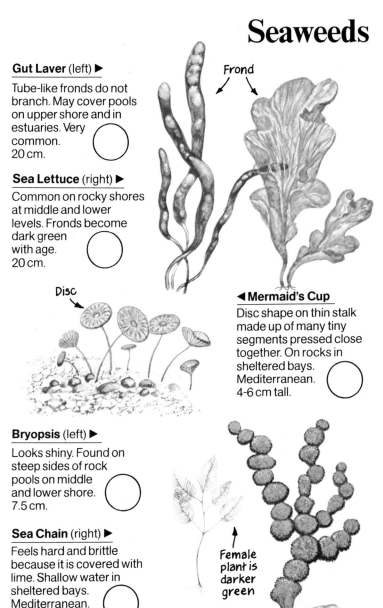

Gut Laver (left) ▶

Tube-like fronds do not branch. May cover pools on upper shore and in estuaries. Very common.
20 cm.

Sea Lettuce (right) ▶

Common on rocky shores at middle and lower levels. Fronds become dark green with age.
20 cm.

Frond

Disc

◀ **Mermaid's Cup**

Disc shape on thin stalk made up of many tiny segments pressed close together. On rocks in sheltered bays. Mediterranean.
4-6 cm tall.

Bryopsis (left) ▶

Looks shiny. Found on steep sides of rock pools on middle and lower shore.
7.5 cm.

Sea Chain (right) ▶

Feels hard and brittle because it is covered with lime. Shallow water in sheltered bays. Mediterranean.
15 cm.

Female plant is darker green

11

Many seaweeds live on the shore, especially on rocky shores. Some can live in and out of the water as the tide comes in and goes out.

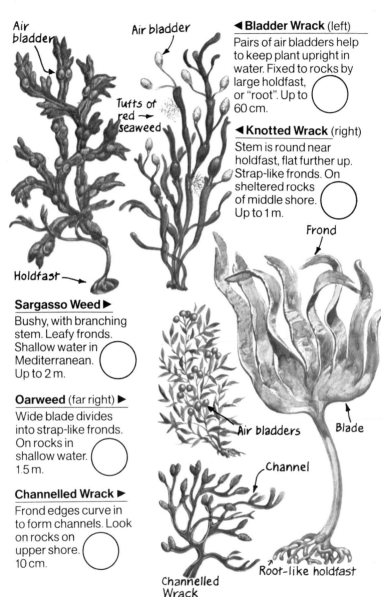

◄ Bladder Wrack (left)
Pairs of air bladders help to keep plant upright in water. Fixed to rocks by large holdfast, or "root". Up to 60 cm.

◄ Knotted Wrack (right)
Stem is round near holdfast, flat further up. Strap-like fronds. On sheltered rocks of middle shore. Up to 1 m.

Air bladder

Air bladder

Tufts of red → seaweed

Frond

Holdfast →

Sargasso Weed ►
Bushy, with branching stem. Leafy fronds. Shallow water in Mediterranean. Up to 2 m.

Oarweed (far right) **►**
Wide blade divides into strap-like fronds. On rocks in shallow water. 1.5 m.

Channelled Wrack ►
Frond edges curve in to form channels. Look on rocks on upper shore. 10 cm.

Air bladders

Blade

Channel

Channelled Wrack

Root-like holdfast

Seaweeds

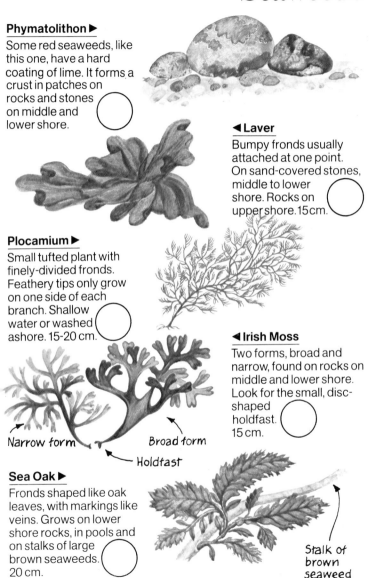

Phymatolithon ▶
Some red seaweeds, like this one, have a hard coating of lime. It forms a crust in patches on rocks and stones on middle and lower shore.

◀ Laver
Bumpy fronds usually attached at one point. On sand-covered stones, middle to lower shore. Rocks on upper shore. 15 cm.

Plocamium ▶
Small tufted plant with finely-divided fronds. Feathery tips only grow on one side of each branch. Shallow water or washed ashore. 15-20 cm.

◀ Irish Moss
Two forms, broad and narrow, found on rocks on middle and lower shore. Look for the small, disc-shaped holdfast. 15 cm.

Narrow form

Broad form

Holdfast

Sea Oak ▶
Fronds shaped like oak leaves, with markings like veins. Grows on lower shore rocks, in pools and on stalks of large brown seaweeds. 20 cm.

Stalk of brown seaweed

Sponges

Sponges are found mostly low down on the shore, usually on rocks. They look like plants, but are really animals.

◄ Scypha ciliata
Shaggy, upright tube, often with fringed top. Lives singly or in clusters in damp, shady places. On stones or among seaweed. Up to 12 cm long.

Polymastia mamillaris ►
Can be orange, pink, or yellowy grey. In shallow water, half-buried in muddy gravel. On stones and shells. Up to 8 cm across.

◄ Sea Orange
Round orange sponge. Surface is grooved. Shallow water, but more often seen offshore. Up to 7 cm across.

Haliclona oculata ►
Looks like a small tree. "Branches" are greyish pink, with openings. Lower shores in fast currents, and estuaries with muddy gravel. Up to 16 cm long.

Regular openings squirt out water

◄ Bread Sponge
Many different shapes, and colour varies from green to yellow. On rocks, shells and seaweed holdfasts. Middle shore and downwards. 10 cm across.

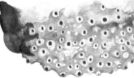

Can be branching shape

Corals

Corals are made up of many tiny animals, called polyps. Their outer skeletons join together to form a large colony.

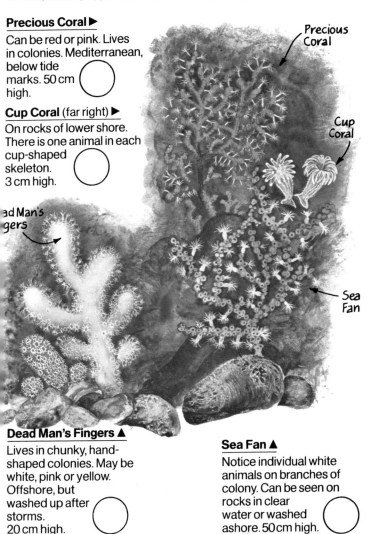

Precious Coral ▶
Can be red or pink. Lives in colonies. Mediterranean, below tide marks. 50 cm high.

Cup Coral (far right) ▶
On rocks of lower shore. There is one animal in each cup-shaped skeleton. 3 cm high.

Dead Man's Fingers

Precious Coral

Cup Coral

Sea Fan

Dead Man's Fingers ▲
Lives in chunky, hand-shaped colonies. May be white, pink or yellow. Offshore, but washed up after storms. 20 cm high.

Sea Fan ▲
Notice individual white animals on branches of colony. Can be seen on rocks in clear water or washed ashore. 50 cm high.

Sea Anemones

These flower-like animals are quite common on rocks, but may be well hidden. When they are not under water their tentacles are drawn in.

Beadlet Anemone ▶

Red or green with a blue spot below each tentacle and a thin blue line round the base.
Common in rock pools. 5 cm high.

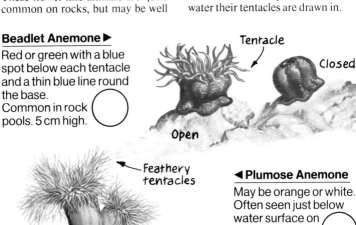

Tentacle

Closed

Open

Feathery tentacles

◀ Plumose Anemone

May be orange or white. Often seen just below water surface on pier supports. 20 cm high.

Snakelocks Anemone ▶

Can be grey or greenish. The sticky tentacles contract when touched, but do not disappear. Rocky shores, sometimes on oarweed. 10 cm across.

◀ Wartlet Anemone

Body varies from green to red, with six rows of white warts and striped tentacles. In lower shore rock pools and crevices. 4 cm across.

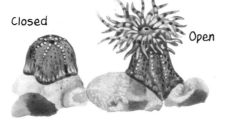

Closed

Open

Sea Anemones

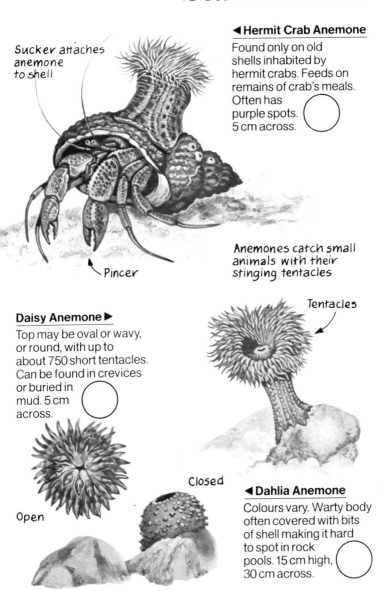

Sucker attaches
anemone
to shell

Pincer

◀ Hermit Crab Anemone

Found only on old
shells inhabited by
hermit crabs. Feeds on
remains of crab's meals.
Often has
purple spots.
5 cm across.

Anemones catch small
animals with their
stinging tentacles

Tentacles

Daisy Anemone ▶

Top may be oval or wavy,
or round, with up to
about 750 short tentacles.
Can be found in crevices
or buried in
mud. 5 cm
across.

Open

Closed

◀ Dahlia Anemone

Colours vary. Warty body
often covered with bits
of shell making it hard
to spot in rock
pools. 15 cm high,
30 cm across.

Fishes

Notice the shape of a fish's body, its fins, and whether or not it has spines.

Some fishes have barbels, which have taste buds on them.

Shore Clingfish ▶

Clings to rocks with sucker. In pools low down on seaweed-covered shores. Both parents guard golden eggs. 6.5 cm.

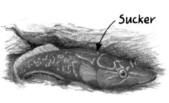

Sucker

◀ Shore Rockling

Rocky shores, in pools and shallow water. Under stones and seaweed. Finds food with its three long barbels. 27 cm.

Barbels

Scorpion Fish ▶

Spines on fin and gill covers are venomous, so do not touch them. Hides in seaweed in shallow water and rock pools. 15 cm.

Venomous spines

◀ Sea Stickleback

Lives among seaweeds in shallow water on rocky, sandy and muddy shores. Builds nest of seaweed where its eggs hatch. 16 cm.

Corkwing Wrasse ▶

Eats animals with shells, which it crushes with its strong teeth. In weedy pools. Colour varies. 26 cm.

Fishes

◀ Montagu's Blenny
Blennies do not have scales. This one lives in bare-sided rock pools. Eats acorn barnacles. 8 cm.

Tompot Blenny ▶
Lives mainly below low tide mark in rock crevices. Male guards eggs, which are laid in small cracks in rock. 30 cm.

◀ Butterfish
Slippery body is flattened sideways. Common among rocks, under seaweed and stones on all kinds of shore. Lays eggs in winter. 25 cm.

Rock Goby ▶
Lives on rocky shores in pools and shallow water, under stones or among seaweed. Lays its eggs under flat stones. 12 cm.

◀ Worm Pipefish
Hides among brown seaweeds, mostly on rocky shores. Male carries eggs under its body until they hatch. 15 cm.

Fishes

Weever ▶
Has very venomous spines. Shuffle your feet when paddling to avoid treading on it. Lies buried in sand in shallow water. 14 cm.

Venomous spines

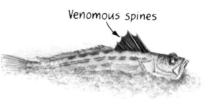

Dorsal fin ──▶

◀ Sand Goby
Like all gobies, has a sucker on underside. Notice dark spot on dorsal fin and blotches on sides. In shoals on sand in shallow water. 9 cm.

Sand-Eel ▶
Swims in large shoals in shallow water. Burrows into sand if alarmed. Often eaten by other fishes, and sea birds. 20 cm.

◀ Dab
Common on sandy and gravelly bottoms, where its colour acts as a camouflage. Feeds on animals with shells, and on worms. 25 cm.

Stargazer ▶
Lies buried in the sand with only its eyes showing. Feeds on small crabs and fishes. Has two venomous spines. Mediterranean. 25 cm.

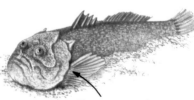

Venomous spines

Fishes

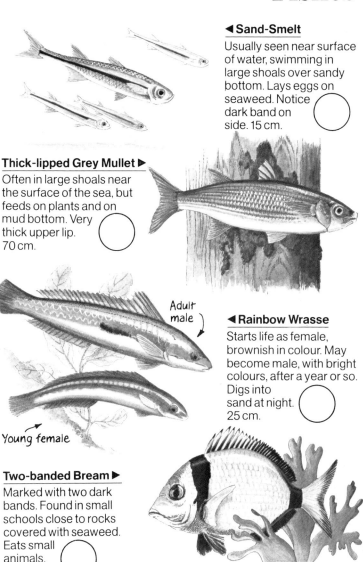

◄ Sand-Smelt
Usually seen near surface of water, swimming in large shoals over sandy bottom. Lays eggs on seaweed. Notice dark band on side. 15 cm.

Thick-lipped Grey Mullet ►
Often in large shoals near the surface of the sea, but feeds on plants and on mud bottom. Very thick upper lip. 70 cm.

Adult male

◄ Rainbow Wrasse
Starts life as female, brownish in colour. May become male, with bright colours, after a year or so. Digs into sand at night. 25 cm.

Young female

Two-banded Bream ►
Marked with two dark bands. Found in small schools close to rocks covered with seaweed. Eats small animals. 30 cm.

Birds

Cormorant (left) ▶

Nests on rocky coasts, especially in the west. Look for the white face patch. 92 cm.

Cormorants and Shags often fly low, close to the water

Shag (right) ▶

Most live on rocky coasts in the west. Crest is visible only in spring. No face patch. 76 cm.

Colourful beak and reddish feet in summer

◀ Puffin

Nests in holes, usually on grassy cliff tops. More common in the north of Britain. Winters at sea. 30 cm.

Razorbill ▶

Likes to nest in cliff cavities, although a few may live on cliff ledges with Guillemots. Spends winter at sea. 30 cm.

Summer

Winter

Summer

Winter

◀ Guillemot

Large crowded colonies nest on cliff ledges, hundreds of metres above the sea. Guillemots spend the winter out at sea. 42 cm.

Birds

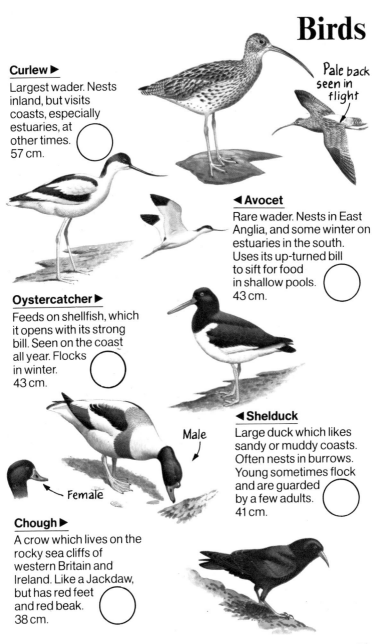

Curlew ▶
Largest wader. Nests inland, but visits coasts, especially estuaries, at other times.
57 cm.

Pale back seen in flight

◀ Avocet
Rare wader. Nests in East Anglia, and some winter on estuaries in the south. Uses its up-turned bill to sift for food in shallow pools.
43 cm.

Oystercatcher ▶
Feeds on shellfish, which it opens with its strong bill. Seen on the coast all year. Flocks in winter.
43 cm.

Male

Female

◀ Shelduck
Large duck which likes sandy or muddy coasts. Often nests in burrows. Young sometimes flock and are guarded by a few adults.
41 cm.

Chough ▶
A crow which lives on the rocky sea cliffs of western Britain and Ireland. Like a Jackdaw, but has red feet and red beak.
38 cm.

Birds

◄ Great Black-backed Gull
Look for its black back
and pale legs. Usually
seen alone or in small
numbers. Will kill and
eat smaller birds.
66 cm.

Lesser Black-backed Gull ►
Although some spend the
winter in Britain, most
are summer visitors. Often
seen inland. Dark grey
back and yellow
legs in summer.
53 cm.

◄ Herring Gull
Found near most coasts.
Nests in colonies on cliffs,
or sometimes on houses.
Grey streaks on
head in winter.
56 cm.

Black-headed Gull ►
Small gull. Dark brown
head in summer; small dark
blotch on head in winter.
Red beak and legs all year
round. Also
common inland.
37 cm.

Summer

Winter

◄ Common Tern
Nest in large groups on
beaches and sand dunes.
Notice the long wings
and tail streamers
in flight. Summer
visitor. 34 cm.

Birds

◀ Little Tern
A summer visitor to
Britain which nests in
small groups on shingle
beaches. Dives
for fish.
24 cm.

Rock Dove ▶
Town pigeons are
descended from these
birds. Usually seen
in small groups
on sea cliffs.
33 cm.

Young

◀ Ringed Plover
Small plump wader with
short bill. Runs along
sandy and shingle beaches,
tilting over to feed.
All year round
in Britain.
19 cm.

Dunlin ▶
Plumage varies between
grey and brown. Feeds in
flocks on sandy beaches.
Down-curved beak.
Mainly a winter
visitor.
19 cm.

Winter

Summer

◀ Redshank
Named after its orange-
red legs. White back and
hind wing edges in flight.
Estuaries and
muddy shores all
year round. 28 cm.

Seals, Otter

All these mammals are very good swimmers, but most seals are rather clumsy on land. Otters are active at night, seals during the day.

Mediterranean Monk Seal ▶

Lives on small rocky beaches on islands. Feeds on fish. It is rare, and the only seal found in the Mediterranean. Not in Britain. 3 m.

Look on sandbanks

◀ Common Seal

Colour varies, but always spotty when adult. Lives in herds on sandbanks, in estuaries. Fast swimmer, and dives for up to 20 to 30 minutes. 1.8 m.

Grey Seal ▶

Lives in small herds on rocky shores. Rests on land at low tide and at sunset, but also sleeps in water. Shy animal. 2.9 m.

When they swim only their heads show above the water

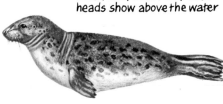

Look for webbed footprints

◀ Otter

Sometimes found in sea or estuaries, but more often near fresh water. Swims well, with long thick tail and webbed feet. Mainly active at night. 1.25 m.

Whales

These mammals are all whales and breathe air. They have a blow-hole on top of their heads for taking in air.

◄ Common Porpoise

Small, toothed whale with blunt snout. Often swims near the coast, in small schools. Eats herring and other fish. 1.8 m.

Bottle-nosed Dolphin ►

In schools of up to several hundred dolphins often near coast. Often swims near boats. Likes jumping high out of the water. 3.6 m.

Beak

◄ Common Dolphin

Has slim body and long, narrow beak. Swims fast, up to 40 kph. Playful and may jump right out of water. In large schools. Seen around ships. 2.4 m.

Lesser Rorqual ►

Small whale with baleen plates instead of teeth. About 50 grooves on the throat. Feeds on small fish and plankton. 9.1 m.

Grooves

◄ White-beaked Dolphin

May be in schools of up to 1,500 dolphins. Looks like Bottle-nosed Dolphin, but more striking. Short, whitish beak. 3 m.

Molluscs

These animals have a hard shell on the outside which protects their soft bodies. Some molluscs live on the seashore. Others live in the sea, but you may find their empty shells washed ashore. Single shells are called univalves. Molluscs that have two shells joined together by muscles, such as cockles, are called bivalves. The empty bivalve shells you find on the beach have often been broken in half by the sea.

Foot is under shell

◄ Common Limpet
Clings to rock with muscular foot. Feeds on seaweed at night. Common on rocky shores. 7 cm long.

Slipper Limpet ►
Often attached to each other in chains, with females at the bottom and males on top. 2.5 cm wide.

◄ Common Mussel
On rocky shores and in estuaries, attached to rocks by thin threads. People collect mussels to eat. 1-10 cm long.

Dog Whelk ►
Common in rock crevices on barnacles. Colour depends on what food it eats. 3 cm high.

◄ Common Periwinkle
Look for it close to the sea on all kinds of shores. Feeds on seaweed. 2.5 cm high.

Molluscs

Common Cerith ▶

On stones, or buried in sand or mud. Hermit crabs use empty shells. Mediterranean. 4.5 cm high.

Painted Topshell ▶

On rocks and under stones. Can be yellow or pink, with red stripes. 2.5 cm high.

Saddle Oyster ▶

Sticks firmly to rocks. Shell often follows shape of rock. Middle shore and below. 6 cm wide.

◀ Dove Shell

Found on rocks in shallow water. Colour varies. Look for empty shells on the beach. Mediterranean. 4.5 cm high.

◀ Netted Dog Whelk

At or below low tide level on rocky shores. Likes sandy crevices. 2.5 cm high.

Mother of pearl ↘

◀ Fool's Cap

Usually in deep water, but may be attached to other shells or rocks low down on the shore. 1.2 cm wide.

Molluscs

Nun Cowrie ▶
Look under stones and in crevices in rocks.
1 cm long.

Ribs →

White Piddock ▶
Burrows into soft rock, wood and firm sand. Found on lower shore.
15 cm long.

Sting Winkle ▶
Drills a hole in oyster shells to eat the flesh inside.
6 cm high.

Dark spots on top of shell

◀ File Shell
White shell with scaly ribs. In rocks crevices and under stones.
Mediterranean.
5 cm long.

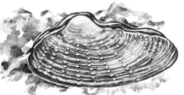

◀ Common Oyster
Shell shape varies and two halves are not the same. In shallow and deep water.
10 cm long.

◀ Common Whelk
Very common on rocky and sandy beaches. Lower shore.
8 cm high.

Molluscs

Great Topshell ▶
Usually lives in water about 10 m deep, but empty shells are often washed up on shore. Notice reddish zig-zag stripes.
2 cm high.

◀ Variegated Scallop
Can be many different colours. One "ear" is twice as long as the other. Very low down on shore.
6 cm long.

Ear

Lurid Cowrie ▶
On muddy and sandy bottoms, often in very deep water. May be washed ashore in the Mediterranean.
5 cm long.

◀ Dog Cockle
Large thick shell with brown markings. Burrows just below the surface of sand.
6.5 cm long.

Heart Cockle ▶
Look at shell from its side to see heart shape. Lives in muddy sand below low tide level, but may be washed ashore.
9.5 cm wide.

Molluscs

◀ Necklace Shell
Preys on other molluscs. Bores a neat hole in shells and eats flesh inside. On sandy shores. 3 cm high.

Wing Oyster ▶
Named after its shape. Attached to stones in deeper waters of the Mediterranean and Atlantic. Uncommon. 7 cm long.

◀ Common Wentletrap
Look for raised ribs. Usually in deep water, sometimes on rocks on shore. Up to 4 cm high.

Pilgrim's Scallop ▶
One of the largest Mediterranean bivalves. Swims by clapping valves together. Used for making spoons and cups. 13 cm wide.

◀ Mediterranean Tun
Eats other molluscs. Deep water or washed up on shore. 25 cm high.

Molluscs

Razor Shell ▶
Looks like an old-fashioned razor. Lives buried in sand or mud, often 1m down. 15 cm long.

◀ Smooth Venus
Pretty, shiny shell. Lives buried in sand or mud on all Mediterranean and some British shores. 11 cm long.

Baltic Tellin ▶
Eaten by many fish, especially by halibut. Burrows in mud and sand of sea, and salty water of estuaries. 2 cm long.

◀ Elephant's Tusk
Named for its shape. Lives in muddy sand of deeper water of Atlantic Ocean, English Channel and North Sea. 5 cm long.

Trough Shell ▶
People catch them for food. Likes to burrow in clean sand or gravel of lower shores. Widespread. 5 cm long.

Molluscs

◄ Edible Cockle
Very common. Burrows in sand or mud from the lower shore down. Often dug up for food.
5 cm wide.

Screw Shell ►
Long thin shell often found in large numbers on sandy bottoms in deep water. Empty shells are sometimes washed ashore.
6 cm high.

◄ Banded Wedge Shell
Named after band markings. Burrows in the sand on the shore and in water up to 10 m deep. Empty shells often found on the beach.
3.5 cm long.

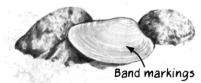

Band markings

Pelican's Foot ►
Its unusual shape makes this shell easy to spot. Large numbers live together on all kinds of seabed.
5.5 cm high.

◄ Common Sand Gaper
So called because two halves of the shell gape when closed. Lives in sand and burrows deeper as it grows. larger.
12 cm wide.

Molluscs

Chink Shell ▶
Usually in shallow water,
on seaweeds.
Striped.
1 cm high.

◀ Blue-rayed Limpet
Rows of blue spots are
bright on young shells,
faded on old ones. On
brown seaweeds
and holdfasts.
1.5 cm long.

Mediterranean Cone ▶
Do not touch. Has tooth
filled with poison to
catch prey.
Mediterranean.
Up to 5 cm high.

◀ Horse Mussel
Usually on oarweed from
lower shore to very deep
water. One of Europe's
largest
mussels.
Up to 20 cm long.

Flat Periwinkle ▶
Colours vary. Feeds on wrack
seaweeds. In rock
pools. Common.
1 cm high.

◀ Pheasant Shell
Found mostly on red
seaweeds in rock pools of
lower shore.
The shell is
glossy.
8 mm high.

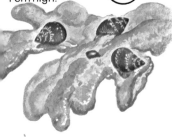

Sea Urchins and Brittle Star

These animals have spiny skins, and rows of suckers which they use for pulling themselves along and for holding on to rocks.

Brown Serpent-star ▶

Stripes on arms darken with age.
Mediterranean.
10-15 cm across.

◀ Small Purple-tipped
Sea Urchin

Under rocks and stones on lower shore. Atlantic coasts. Spines have purple tips.
Up to 4 cm across.

Edible Sea Urchin ▶

On rocky shores in west Britain, but becoming rare. Spines drop off when sea urchins die. Shell is called a test.
Up to 15 cm across.

Test

Live Sea Urchin

◀ Common Mediterranean
Sea Urchin (left)

Holds bits of seaweed or shell over itself.
Not in Britain.
Up to 10 cm across.

◀ Black Sea Urchin (right)

Black spines. Lower shore and deep water.
Not in Britain.
6-10 cm across.

Sea Potato ▶

Sea urchin that lives in sand at lowest tide level. Leaves a dent on surface where it has burrowed. Empty tests may be washed ashore in storms.
5-6 cm long.

Test

Starfishes and Brittle Stars

Sunstar

Cushion Starlet

◄ Sunstar

Preys on other starfish. Spiny, with up to 15 arms. Often beautifully patterned. Mostly North Sea and Channel coasts. 4-8 cm across.

Common Starfish

Has five arms, like most starfishes. Tips often turn up when starfish moves. Up to 50 cm across, but those on shore only 5-10 cm.

Common Starfish

Cushion Starlet

Very small starfish with short arms. Likes shady parts of rock pools. West coast. 1-2 cm across.

Mediterranean Multi-armed

Starfish (far right) ►

6-8 arms, often of different lengths. 8-12 cm across.

Mediterranean Multi-armed Starfish

◄ Spiny Starfish

On rocky Mediterranean and Atlantic coasts, low down on shore and in deep water. Large spines. Inshore. 8-12 cm across.

Spiny Starfish

Small Brittle Star ►

Very common, but hard to spot. Under stones. 3 cm across.

Common Brittle Star ►

Very fragile, so handle gently. Under stones. 3-8 cm across.

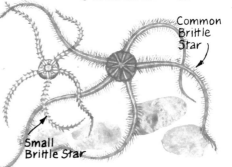

Common Brittle Star

Small Brittle Star

Crustaceans

A large group of animals that have shells which protect them.

◄ Acorn Barnacle
Very common on rocks. Often has one broad plate. Its opening is diamond-shaped.
1.5 cm long.

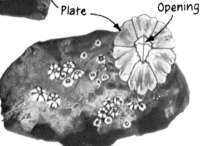

Opening

Plate

Star Barnacle ►
Look on rocks. In the south it may be found near Acorn Barnacle, but higher up the beach. The opening is kite-shaped.
1.2 cm long.

◄ Beach Hopper
Jumps about when disturbed. Lives under stones and among seaweed high up on beach. Male has claws on second pair of legs. 2 cm long.

Sea Scud ►
Lives on muddy sand and in sheltered estuaries. Hides under stones on middle and lower shore.
1.3 cm long.

Claw

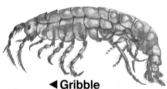

◄ Gribble
Lives in wood. Look for the tiny holes it bores into piers and in the hulls of boats.
4 mm long.

Crustaceans

Sea Slater ▶

Look in cracks in breakwaters and on rocks above high tide level. Moves down shore to feed as tide goes out. Runs fast. 2.5 cm long.

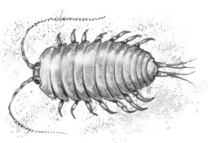

◀ Chameleon Prawn

Usually lives in deep water, but may be found among seaweed in lower shore rock pools. Changes colour to match seaweed. 2.5 cm long.

White Shrimp ▶

Common in rock pools on lower shore and in shallow water in sandy estuaries. 5 cm long.

◀ Common Prawn

Common in shallow water, sometimes found in rock pools. Like all prawns and shrimps, its feelers are longer than its body. 6.5 cm long.

Claw

Sand Shrimp ▶

Common in sandy estuaries. Broad flattened claws on first legs. People catch them to eat. 5 cm long.

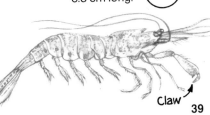

Claw

39

Crustaceans

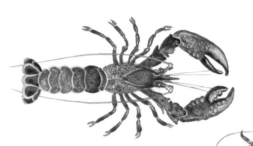

◀ Common Lobster

Small ones sometimes found in lower shore rock pools. It is illegal to take any less than 8 cm long. Strong pincers on front legs are slightly unequal. Up to 45 cm long.

Montagu's Plated Lobster ▶

Its last pair of legs are hidden under its body. Found under seaweed and stones. 4 cm long.

◀ Broad-clawed Porcelain Crab

Notice broad, hairy claws and very small back legs. Under stones. Middle and lower shores. 1.2 cm long.

Long-clawed Porcelain Crab ▶

Long claws are not hairy. Can be found among stones and on oarweed holdfasts on lower shore. 1.2 cm long.

Shell of Common Whelk

◀ Common Hermit Crab

Has no hard shell of its own to protect soft body so lives in empty shell like this one. In rock pools. Up to 10 cm long.

Crustaceans

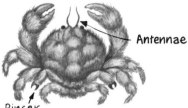

Sponge Crab ▶

Covered in hairs and looks furry. Often carries piece of sponge on its back, held by last two pairs of legs. In rock pools. Rare. 7 cm long.

Antennae

Pincer

◀ Shore Crab

Has smooth, broad shell. Young ones often have attractive markings. Common on sandy and rocky shores. 4 cm long.

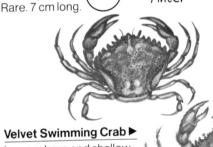

Velvet Swimming Crab ▶

Lower shore and shallow water. Red eyes, with 8-10 small points in between, on shell edge. Hairy shell. 8 cm long.

Broad back legs act as swimming paddles

◀ Pennant's Crab

Has long, smooth shell, and swimming paddles on last pair of legs. Swims near sandy bottom in shallow water. Burrows fast. 3.5 cm long.

Hairy Crab ▶

Has wide, hairy body and large, unequal pincers. Common in some places, and found among stones and seaweed. Lower shore. 2 cm long.

Crustaceans

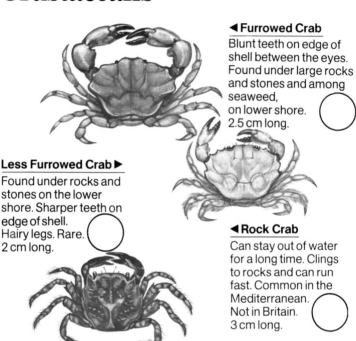

◀ Furrowed Crab
Blunt teeth on edge of shell between the eyes. Found under large rocks and stones and among seaweed, on lower shore. 2.5 cm long.

Less Furrowed Crab ▶
Found under rocks and stones on the lower shore. Sharper teeth on edge of shell. Hairy legs. Rare. 2 cm long.

◀ Rock Crab
Can stay out of water for a long time. Clings to rocks and can run fast. Common in the Mediterranean. Not in Britain. 3 cm long.

Edible Crab ▶
Large ones found in deep water, but small ones common in rock pools, under rocks and buried in sand on lower shore. Up to 11.5 cm long.

◀ Toothed Pirimela
Looks like young shore crab, but has larger teeth on shell edge, and front edge is more pointed. 1 cm long.

Crustaceans

Thornback Spider Crab ▶

Shell is oval and spiny. Often caught in lobster pots. Sometimes in rock pools on lower shore, and in oarweed. 15 cm long.

Beak

◀ Slender-legged Spider Crab

Notice long beak. Often has bits of seaweed or sponge on shell. Moves slowly. Rock pools. 1.8 cm long.

Toad Crab ▶

Pear-shaped shell often covered with sponges and seaweed. Eyes can be withdrawn into sockets. Lower shore rock pools. 10 cm long.

Common Mussel

◀ Pea Crab

Lives inside bivalve shells. Female is large and soft; male small with hard shell. Up to 1.2 cm long.

Jellyfishes

These animals are not all real jelly-fishes, but are closely related. Most live in the sea, but you may see them washed ashore on the beach.

Sail

Float

◀ Portuguese Man-o'-War

Really a colony of many tiny individuals living together. Floats on the sea, but sometimes washed ashore. Do not touch: the tentacles can give painful stings. Float 15 cm long.

Tentacles up to 20m long

By-the-Wind Sailor ▶

May be blown ashore in winds. Sometimes in shoals.
Harmless. Float 3 cm across.

Purple crescents

◀ Moon Jellyfish

Very common on all coasts of Europe and in all oceans of the world. Harmless. Transparent with purple rim and crescents. Up to 15 cm across.

Four tentacles hang underneath

Aequorea ▶

Lives in open sea, but often washed up on the beach. Common in late summer.
Harmless. Up to 15 cm across.

Jellyfishes

ion's Mane Jellyfish ▶

his honey-coloured kind
s harmless, but a related
lue kind stings badly.
3oth found in Europe,
articularly the
orth. Up to 2 m
cross.

Lobed edge

Stalked Jellyfish ▼

Does not swim. Body has
eight tufts of tentacles
round rim. On seaweeds on
shore. Harmless.
Body is 5 mm
high.

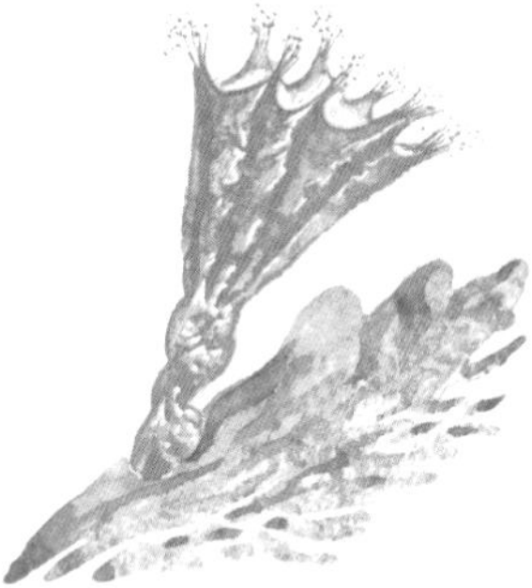

Pelagia ▲

Body is mushroom-shaped
and has warty surface.
Thick tentacles can give
painful stings. Lives in
open sea, rarely
near coast.
10 cm across.

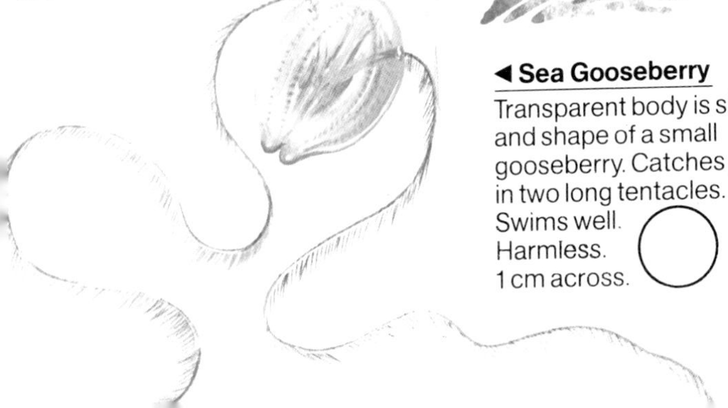

◀ Sea Gooseberry

Transparent body is size
and shape of a small
gooseberry. Catches prey
in two long tentacles.
Swims well.
Harmless.
1 cm across.

45

Worms

There are many kinds of worms that live on the shore. Some live in tubes of sand, others burrow in the sand or move on the surface.

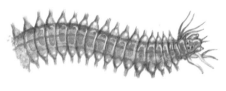

◄ Ragworm
Burrows in sand and mud. Bristles along each side and red line down back. From middle shore to shallow water. 10 cm long.

Lugworm ►
Fat worm with thin tail. Lives buried in sand. Sand casts and hollows show where two ends of its burrow are. 15 cm long.

Gills for breathing

Worm in tube

◄ Sand Mason
Long thin worm that lives in a tube buried in the sand. Tip of tube, made of sand and shell bits, sticks up above surface. 20 cm long.

Green Leaf Worm ►
Crawls among barnacles and under seaweed on rocks, or hides in rock crevices. Upper shore to shallow water. 10 cm long.

◄ Keelworm
Worm lives in hard white tube that has a ridge along the top. Look for the tubes on rocks, stones and empty shells. Up to 3 cm long.

Cuttlefish, Octopus, Squids

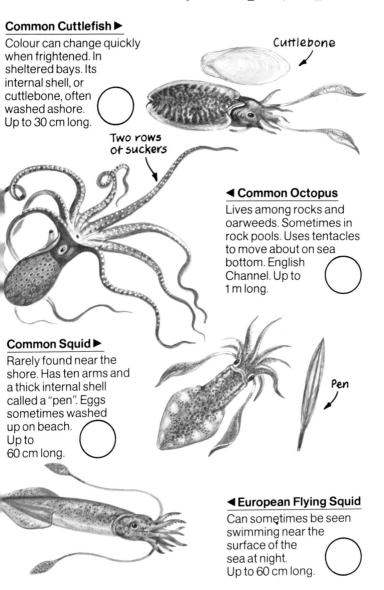

Common Cuttlefish ▶

Colour can change quickly when frightened. In sheltered bays. Its internal shell, or cuttlebone, often washed ashore. Up to 30 cm long.

Cuttlebone

Two rows of suckers

◀ Common Octopus

Lives among rocks and oarweeds. Sometimes in rock pools. Uses tentacles to move about on sea bottom. English Channel. Up to 1 m long.

Common Squid ▶

Rarely found near the shore. Has ten arms and a thick internal shell called a "pen". Eggs sometimes washed up on beach. Up to 60 cm long.

Pen

◀ European Flying Squid

Can sometimes be seen swimming near the surface of the sea at night. Up to 60 cm long.

Sea Slugs

Sea slugs are molluscs that have no shells. They have tentacles on their heads and are often brightly coloured.

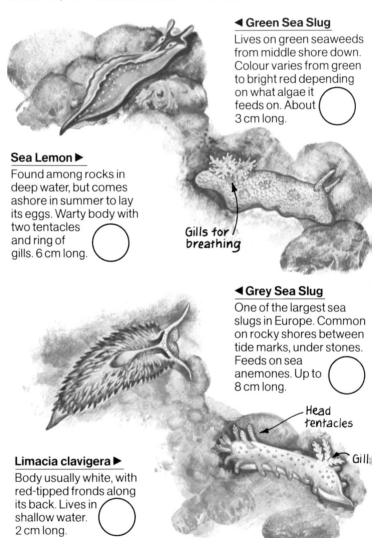

◀ Green Sea Slug

Lives on green seaweeds from middle shore down. Colour varies from green to bright red depending on what algae it feeds on. About 3 cm long.

Sea Lemon ▶

Found among rocks in deep water, but comes ashore in summer to lay its eggs. Warty body with two tentacles and ring of gills. 6 cm long.

Gills for breathing

◀ Grey Sea Slug

One of the largest sea slugs in Europe. Common on rocky shores between tide marks, under stones. Feeds on sea anemones. Up to 8 cm long.

Head tentacles

Gill

Limacia clavigera ▶

Body usually white, with red-tipped fronds along its back. Lives in shallow water. 2 cm long.

Marks in the Sand

A sandy beach may look empty, but look closely for signs like these left by seashore animals. Their tracks show up best in wet sand.

Look for the pointed claws of gulls' tracks. The webbing shows only in soft, wet sand.

The Sand Mason lives in the sand in a tube of shell bits. The top of the tube and fringed tip of the worm stick up out of the sand.

The Sea Potato leaves a dent in the sand where it burrows.

A tern's tracks are small, with very narrow webbing.

Sand casts and hollows show at the openings of a Lugworm's burrow.

Where Do the Shells Live?

Where would you look for these shells on the beach? Write the number of each shell on the line by the correct place. The answers are upside-down at the bottom of the opposite page.

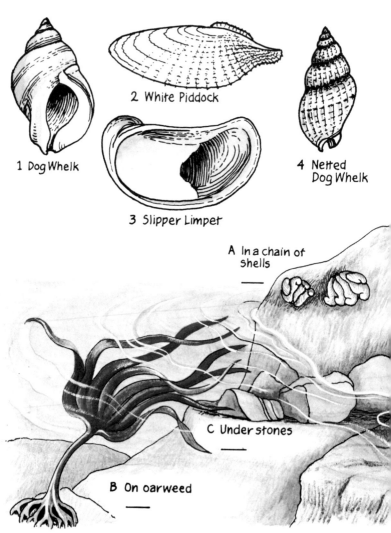

2 White Piddock

1 Dog Whelk

3 Slipper Limpet

4 Netted Dog Whelk

A In a chain of shells
___

C Under stones
___

B On oarweed
___

50

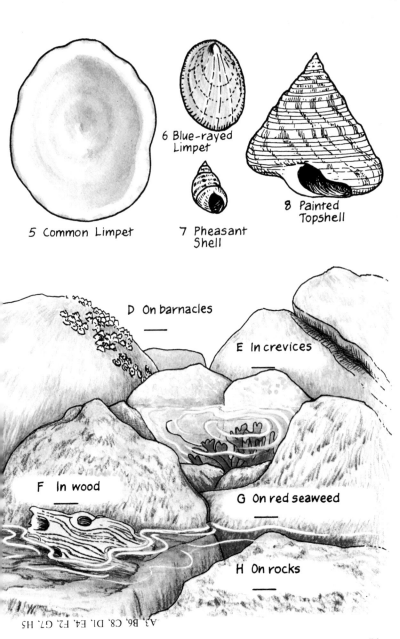

5 Common Limpet

6 Blue-rayed Limpet

7 Pheasant Shell

8 Painted Topshell

D On barnacles ___

E In crevices ___

F In wood ___

G On red seaweed ___

H On rocks ___

A3, B6, C8, D1, E4, F2, G7, H5

Name the Birds

How many of these birds can you identify? Write their names on the lines. The answers are upside-down at the bottom of the opposite page.

1 _____

2 _____

3 _____

4 _____

5 _____

6 _____

7 _____

8 _____

9 _____

10 _____

1. Curlew 2. Avocet 3. Shelduck 4. Oystercatcher
5. Razorbill 6. Puffin 7. Black-headed Gull 8. Cormorant
9. Ringed Plover 10. Common Tern

Rock Pool Quiz

Some of the plants and animals found in rock pools also live elsewhere on the beach and can survive out of water at low tide. Others need to be in the water all the time. Search for them under seaweed and stones. Can you name the things living in this pool? The answers are upside-down at the bottom of the opposite page.

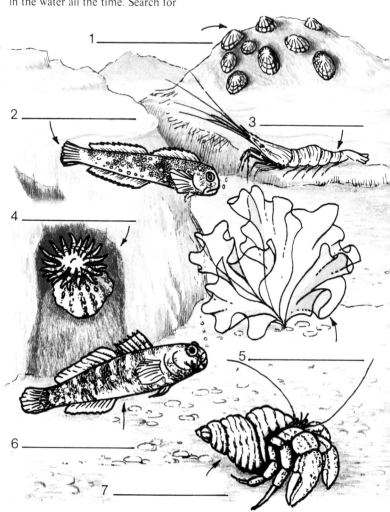

1 _____

2 _____

3 _____

4 _____

5 _____

6 _____

7 _____

Close-up

8 _____

9 _____

10 _____

11 _____

12 _____

13 _____

14 _____

1. Common Limpet 2. Montagu's Blenny 3. Common Prawn 4. Wartlet Anemon…
5. Sea Lettuce 6. Rock Goby 7. Hermit Crab 8. Acorn Barnacles 9. Dog Whelks
10. Beadlet Anemone 11. Common Lobster 12. Cushion Starlet 13. Corkwing Wra…
14. Edible Crab

Collecting Shells

Collect your shells in a plastic bag as you walk along the beach. Look under rocks and seaweed too. Be sure not to take any shells that still have live animals inside them. Here are some ideas for things to do with your shells. Clean them first in warm water.

Make a Display Case

Take off the tops of large empty matchboxes and glue the boxes together like this. Put one shell into each box with a piece of paper giving its name and where and when you found it.

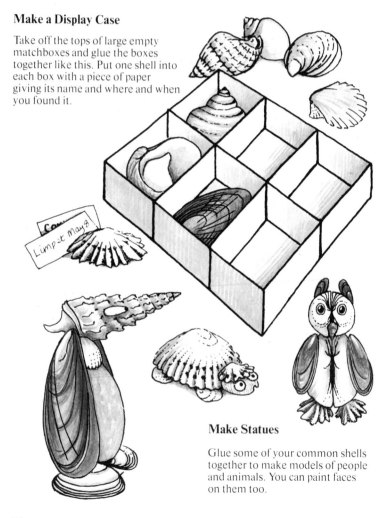

Make Statues

Glue some of your common shells together to make models of people and animals. You can paint faces on them too.

Make Pictures

Draw a simple picture on a piece of cardboard. Glue small, common shells on to it, filling in the shape you have drawn.

Cardboard

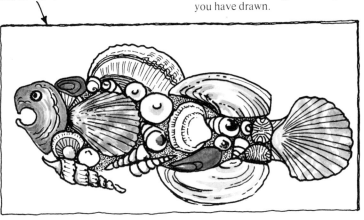

Make Models

Pick out some shells whose shapes remind you of other things. Paint them so that they look as you imagined them.

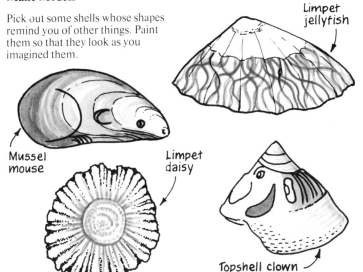

Limpet jellyfish

Mussel mouse

Limpet daisy

Topshell clown

Books to Read

The NatureTrail Book of Seashore Life. Su Swallow (Usborne)
Seashore Life on Rocky Shores.
Seashore Life on Sandy Beaches.
Sea Shells of the Seashore. Life of our Seas. Heather Angel (Jarrold paperbacks)
Seashore. Ian Murray (A. & C. Black)
Creatures of the Bay. Christopher Reynolds (hardback Andre Deutsch/paperback Target)
The Hamlyn Guide to the Seashore and Shallow Seas of Britain and Europe. A. C. Campbell (Hamlyn)

Collins Pocket Guide to the Sea Shore. John Barrett and C. M. Yonge (Collins)
A Field Guide to the Mediterranean Sea Shore. W. Luther and K. Siedler (Collins)
Collins Guide to the Sea Fishes of Britain and North-West Europe. B. J. Muus, P. Dahlstrom (Collins)
Spotter's Guide to Birds. Peter Holden (Usborne)
The Oxford Book of Invertebrates. D. Nichols, J. Cooke and D. Whiteley (OUP)

Index

Scorecard

The animals and plants in this scorecard are arranged in alphabetical order. When you spot one of them, fill in the date next to the name of the animal or plant. You can also add up your score after a day out spotting.

	Score	Date seen		Score	Date seen
Anemone, Beadlet	5		Campion, Sea	5	
Anemone, Dahlia	15		Centaury, Sea	20	
Anemone, Daisy	20		Cerith, Common	25	
Anemone, Hermit Crab	15		Chough	25	
Anemone, Plumose	15		Clingfish, Shore	25	
Anemone, Snakelocks	10		Cockle, Dog	10	
Anemone, Wartlet	20		Cockle, Edible	5	
Arrow-Grass, Sea	10		Cockle, Heart	20	
Aster, Sea	20		Cone, Mediterranean	25	
Avocet	25		Coral, Cup	15	
Barnacle, Acorn	5		Coral, Precious	20	
Barnacle, Star	5		Cormorant	15	
Beach Hopper	5		Cowrie, Lurid	25	
Bindweed, Sea	10		Cowrie, Nun	15	
Blenny, Montagu's	15		Crab, Broad-clawed Porcelain	5	
Blenny, Tompot	10		Crab, Common Hermit	5	
Bream, Two-banded	25		Crab, Edible	5	
Brittle Star, Common	5		Crab, Furrowed	20	
Brittle Star, Small	5		Crab, Hairy	15	
Bryopsis	15		Crab, Less Furrowed	20	
Butterfish	5		Crab, Long-clawed Porcelain	5	

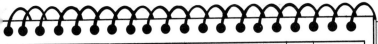

	Score	Date seen		Score	Date seen
Crab, Pea	20		Guillemot	15	
Crab, Pennant's	10		Gull, Black-headed	5	
Crab, Rock	25		Gull, Great Black-backed	10	
Crab, Shore	5		Gull, Herring	5	
Crab, Slender-legged Spider	15		Gull, Lesser Black-backed	10	
Crab, Sponge	25		Haliclona oculata	15	
Crab, Thornback Spider	10		Holly, Sea	15	
Crab, Toad	10		Irish Moss	10	
Crab, Toothed Pirimela	25		Jellyfish, Aequorea	10	
Crab, Velvet Swimming	5		Jellyfish, By-the-Wind Sailor	20	
Curlew	10		Jellyfish, Lion's Mane	25	
Cuttlefish, Common	5		Jellyfish, Moon	5	
Dab	5		Jellyfish, Pelagia	25	
Dead Man's Fingers	10		Jellyfish, Portuguese Man-o'-War	20	
Dolphin, Bottle-nosed	25		Jellyfish, Stalked	20	
Dolphin, Common	20		Kale, Sea	25	
Dolphin, White-beaked	25		Keelworm	5	
Dove, Rock	25		Lavender, Sea	10	
Dunlin	25		Laver	10	
Eel, Sand	5		Laver, Gut	5	
Elephant's Tusk	15		Limacia clavigera	20	
Fool's Cap	15		Limpet, Blue-rayed	15	
Goby, Rock	10		Limpet, Common	5	
Goby, Sand	5		Limpet, Slipper	5	
Gribble	10		Lobster, Common	20	

	Score	Date seen		Score	Date seen
Lobster, Montagu's Plated	10		Polymastia mamillaris	15	
Lugworm	5		Poppy, Yellow Horned	15	
Marram Grass	15		Porpoise, Common	20	
Mayweed, Sea	10		Prawn, Chameleon	10	
Mermaid's Cup	25		Prawn, Common	5	
Milkwort, Sea	10		Puffin	20	
Mullet, Thick-lipped Grey	10		Ragworm	5	
Mussel, Common	5		Razorbill	15	
Mussel, Horse	10		Redshank	10	
Oarweed	15		Rockling, Shore	15	
Octopus, Common	15		Rorqual, Lesser	25	
Otter	15		Samphire, Golden	15	
Oyster, Saddle	15		Sand Gaper, Common	10	
Oyster, Common	5		Sand Mason	10	
Oyster, Wing	15		Sandwort, Sea	10	
Oystercatcher	10		Sargasso Weed	20	
Pelican's Foot	20		Scallop, Pilgrim's	25	
Periwinkle, Common	5		Scallop, Variegated	10	
Periwinkle, Flat	5		Scorpion Fish	20	
Phymatolithon	15		Scypha ciliata	5	
Piddock, White	15		Seablite, Annual	15	
Pipefish, Worm	15		Sea Chain	25	
Plantain, Buckshorn	15		Sea Fan	20	
Plocamium	15		Sea Gooseberry	20	
Plover, Ringed	5		Seal, Common	10	

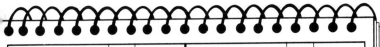

	Score	Date seen		Score	Date seen
Seal, Grey	15		Shell, Trough	5	
Seal, Mediterranean Monk	25		Shrimp, Sand	5	
Sea Lemon	10		Shrimp, White	5	
Sea Lettuce	5		Slater, Sea	5	
Sea Oak	20		Smelt, Sand	10	
Sea Orange	20		Smooth Venus	20	
Sea Potato	15		Sponge, Bread	10	
Sea Scud	5		Squid, Common	20	
Sea Slug, Green	15		Squid, European Flying	25	
Sea Slug, Grey	10		Starfish, Common	5	
Sea Urchin, Black	15		Starfish, Cushion Starlet	5	
Sea Urchin, Common Mediterranean	5		Starfish, Med. Multi-armed	10	
Sea Urchin, Edible	10		Starfish, Spiny	10	
Sea Urchin, Small Purple-tipped	5		Starfish, Sunstar	10	
Serpent-star, Brown	5		Stargazer	25	
Shag	15		Stickleback, Sea	10	
Shelduck	10		Tellin, Baltic	5	
Shell, Banded Wedge	5		Tern, Common	10	
Shell, Chink	10		Tern, Little	20	
Shell, Dove	25		Thrift/Sea Pink	5	
Shell, File	25		Topshell, Great	15	
Shell, Necklace	15		Topshell, Painted	10	
Shell, Pheasant	20		Trefoil, Bird's Foot	10	
Shell, Razor	10		Tun, Mediterranean	25	
Shell, Screw	10		Weever	10	

	Score	Date seen		Score	Date seen
Wentletrap, Common	15				
Whelk, Common	5				
Whelk, Dog	5				
Whelk, Netted Dog	10				
Winkle, Sting	20				
Worm, Green Leaf	10				
Wormwood, Sea	15				
Wrack, Bladder	5				
Wrack, Channelled	10				
Wrack, Knotted	5				
Wrasse, Corkwing	10				
Wrasse, Rainbow	25				